D0179120

Chapter One:

The Choir

There was only one window in the dark room. It was tall and thin and curved to a point at the top. Seven-year-old Louis thought the whole place was a bit creepy. An old man wearing a black

cape, a bit like Batman's but much
longer, stood behind a brightly-
polished piano. He looked up
and spoke to Louis' mum.

"So, you've brought Louis to be
auditioned for the cathedral choir?"
he asked her.

Louis' mum nodded. "He's ever such
a good little singer," she said.

The man behind the piano didn't look impressed. He could see Louis fidgeting and looking bored. "Well, I suppose I'd better hear him sing. Have you got your music with you, Louis?"

"Oh, he doesn't use music," Louis' mum explained. "He sings unaccompanied."

The man sighed. "Very well," he muttered.

"Louis!" his mum hissed. But Louis wasn't listening. He was too busy looking out of the tall, thin window where he thought he could see an aeroplane climbing steeply up into the clouds. The truth was, he didn't really understand what all this choir business was about. He was just pleased to have an afternoon off school.

"Louis!" his mum hissed again, more

loudly this time. "Sing for the man!"

So Louis sang.

When he had finished, Louis' mum turned to the man behind the piano and said, "What do you think, then?"

The man slowly smiled. "I think Louis has a most wonderful voice. I'd be delighted to offer him a place in the cathedral choir. I will write to you with full details in a day or so."

Louis' mum beamed. "There you go, Louis," she said. "What did I tell you?"

When they got home, Louis' mum explained everything to him. "You'll go to the cathedral choir school and sing at the cathedral services. Isn't that exciting?"

Louis nodded.

"It's a big decision, but it's *your* decision, Louis. I won't be cross with you if you don't want to go, even though it's a free private education and you'd be on the TV at Christmas singing carols."

"Would I still be able to do gym?" asked Louis. Louis went to gym club after school. It was his favourite thing in the whole world.

Louis' mum shook her head. "No, love, you wouldn't."

Louis looked his mum full in the face. "I don't want to do choir. I want to do gym," he said.

Chapter Two:

The Dream

The gym club was about 42 km from where Louis lived, and four days a week after school his mum drove him all the way there and back. Louis loved being at the gym with his friends, bouncing, somersaulting and doing flips. But there was a problem, a big one: Louis was trouble. He mucked about and couldn't concentrate on anything for very long at all.

Louis' mum took him to a specialist doctor who found out he was suffering from attention deficit hyperactivity disorder, or ADHD. Louis was given a special medicine called Ritalin. Although it helped him to concentrate and do better at gym, he hated it. It made him feel like a zombie. At school he sat in his classroom at lunchtime, too tired to go out and play. When he was thirteen he asked his mum if he could come off Ritalin, and she agreed.

Louis still messed about though. At gym club he kept getting into trouble. When that happened, Paul Hill, his coach, sent him to climb the rope fifty times. What Louis did was to climb it once then sit at the top singing and blowing

dust off the ceiling. So he was given a different kind of punishment: doing circles on the pommel horse.

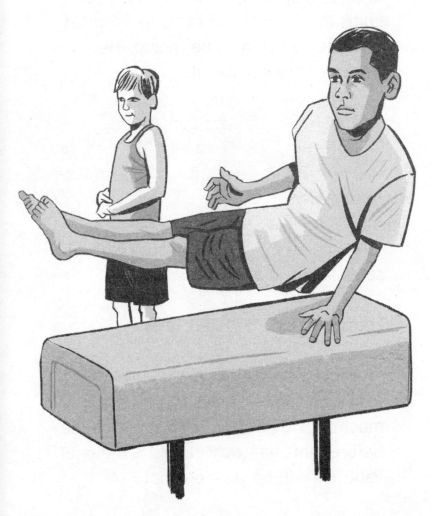

Each time he went on the pommel horse, Louis had to support his bodyweight on his hands. A searing pain would shoot up through his wrists and arms and up into his shoulders. But Louis didn't mind. In fact, he enjoyed working on the pommel horse. He became very good at it.

The man who ran the gym, Terry Sharpington, had been very ill. One day Paul came into the club and took Louis to one side.

"I've got some sad news, Louis," Paul said. "Terry died this morning."

Louis felt sad. He liked Terry.

"I went to see Terry yesterday evening," Paul went on. "He was too ill to say much, but the last thing he said to me before I left him was: 'Louis is the one, Paul. He will be your champion.'"

Louis felt tears sting the back of his eyes. He sat with Paul in silence for a moment. Then he said quietly, "Paul, can I go on the pommel horse, even though I haven't been mucking about?"

Paul nodded. "Yeah, of course you can," he replied.

Louis still had a tendency to muck about, but from that day on he worked hard at the gym.

In 2004, a week before his fifteenth birthday, Louis went to Slovenia to compete in the European Junior Gymnastics Championships. He'd hoped to get through the heats to the final. He did more than that: he won the competition, becoming the European Junior Pommel Horse Champion!

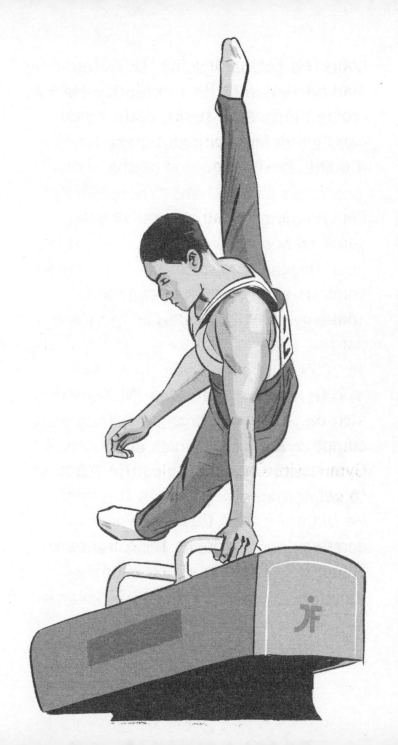

When he got back home, Louis found he had become a bit of a celebrity. He was invited onto *Blue Peter*. After he'd finished doing a pommel horse routine for the TV viewers, one of the producers said to him: "There'll be a lot of young kids out there who will want to become gymnasts after seeing your display, Louis." It was true. Louis' exploits in Slovenia had started to make gymnastics a popular sport.

In 2005, just over a year later, Louis was in his room watching TV. The news was on, live from Singapore. They were about to announce which country had won the honour of staging the 2012 Olympic Games.

In the expectant hush, Louis heard the magical words: "The Games of the thirtieth Olympiad in 2012 are awarded to ... the city of London!"

Louis watched, enthralled, as David Beckham, Seb Coe and Steve Redgrave all leapt about in excitement. At that moment, he realised he had a dream; a dream to win a medal at the London Olympics.

Chapter Three:
Disaster!

Louis sat in the careers teacher's office. The walls were covered in posters advertising different kinds of jobs: engineer, nurse, soldier.

The careers teacher looked up from his desk. "Any idea what you want to do when you leave school, Louis?" he asked.

Louis nodded. "I want to be a gymnast," he said.

The careers teacher sighed. "Oh, come on, Louis. Show some sense, we're not talking about dreams here. We're talking about the real world." He cast his eyes over some leaflets on his desk. "Have you ever thought of becoming an accountant?"

Louis looked at the careers teacher as if he was mad. "No," he replied. "I've never thought of becoming an accountant. For one simple reason: I hate maths!"

While he was in his second year of A-levels, Louis was invited to compete in the Youth Olympic Festival in Sydney, Australia. He won three medals in all, including gold on the pommel horse.

When he got back home, Louis met with the bosses of British Gymnastics. They were very impressed with his medal haul from the Youth Olympics.

"What are you thinking of doing next, Louis?" the head coach asked.

"I want to take part in the proper Olympics," replied Louis. "And I want to win an Olympic medal."

The British Gymnastics bosses laughed. "No one from Britain has won an Olympic medal in gymnastics for a hundred years! What makes you think you can?"

Louis left the meeting feeling angry and fed up. Just a week ago he had been waving to a cheering crowd from the winner's podium at the Youth Olympics. But he would show them: he would prove the old guys at British Gymnastics wrong. He would win an Olympic medal.

Over the next year, Louis worked hard, devoting all of his time to training. His routine on the pommel horse got better and better. In 2007, he won gold at the British Championships and silver at the Glasgow Grand Prix. With these results, Louis was sure he'd get a place in the Team GB gymnastics squad for the Beijing Olympics. There was just one competition left before Beijing: the 2008 European Championships in Switzerland. It was his last chance to show the selectors what he was capable of.

Louis stood beside the pommel horse, as he had done so many times before, waiting to do his routine in the qualifying rounds. He leapt onto the horse, but then just five seconds into his routine he slipped and crashed to the floor. Somehow he managed to get

back onto the horse and finish, but his fall meant he had a low score. He didn't make the cut to the finals.

It was a disaster! Now he wasn't in the finals his chances of being selected for Beijing looked very slim.

Chapter Four:
Making History

Louis' coach Paul Hill tried to console him. "These things can happen to the best athletes, Louis," he said.

Paul's words didn't cheer Louis up at all. He knew he had an agonising wait to see whether he'd made the squad for Beijing.

Weeks later, Louis was taking a break at the gym when his phone rang.

"Hi. Is that Louis?"

"Yeah..."

"I'm calling from Team GB."

This was it. Louis was about to find out whether or not he was going to the Beijing Olympic Games.

"We'd like you to go to Beijing as part of Team GB's gymnastics squad."

"Ye-e-a-a-h!" roared Louis.

Louis was doubly pleased because the other male gymnast in Team GB was Dan Keatings. Dan was younger than

Louis, but trained with him at the same gym in Huntingdon. Louis' mum and Dan's parents flew out to Beijing and rented an apartment together.

Both Louis and Dan were staying in the athletes' village in Beijing. Louis loved it. It was surrounded by fantastic gardens, in the middle of which was a koi carp lake with a bridge and stepping stones across it.

In truth, there wasn't much time for enjoying the scenery and sights of Beijing; Louis was focused on the competition. He did well in the qualifying rounds and made it into the finals.

When the day of the finals eventually came, Louis knew he had to do all he could to keep himself chilled out and calm. On the bus into the stadium he put his headphones on and listened to his favourite reggae music. He had been drawn to go sixth, so he knew there would be a lot of waiting around. He sat on the arena floor with his coat over his head, just soaking up the atmosphere.

When he finally took the floor he looked around the vast arena. He knew roughly where his mum was sitting and he spotted her. She looked nervous, but willing him on to do well.

He leapt onto the pommel horse, desperate not to slip and fall off this time. He held on and performed a solid — though not perfect — routine. The scores flashed up. Louis was in silver medal position!

But there were two gymnasts still to go. If they both scored higher marks than him, Louis knew he would be left without a medal.

The next gymnast up was from Venezuela. Louis watched him mount the pommel horse, then stared in amazement as he slipped and fell off. Louis knew at that moment that he had won an Olympic medal.

In fact, Louis won bronze. At the age of just nineteen he had proved the doubters wrong. He had made history, becoming the first British male gymnast for one hundred years to win an individual medal.

He looked up from the podium to where his mum was sitting and flashed her a big smile. He wasn't sure whether she saw or not; her eyes were full of tears of joy.

Chapter Five:

Team Captain

The London Olympic Games weren't going to be taking place until 2012. That was four years away, but Louis started preparing for them as soon as he got back from Beijing. He knew he had to

be fitter, sharper and able to present the best routine in the world if he was going to win gold.

The training went well. Louis won a silver medal in both the 2009 and the 2010 European Championships. In 2011 he took silver at the World Artistic Gymnastics in Tokyo, Japan. Krisztián Berki from Hungary took gold. Louis was also second behind him in the 2012 European Championships. He knew that Krisztián Berki would be the man he would need to beat at the London Olympics.

For Louis, London 2012 was a very different kind of Olympic experience to Beijing. For a start there were five members of the Team GB men's gymnastics squad. Louis was the only one of them to have competed in an Olympic Games before. He was the eldest and he was the team captain.

Chapter Six:

The Best Routine Ever

The men's gymnastics event was one of the first to be staged. Louis led his team well. They won a bronze medal: the first gymnastics team medal that Britain had won at the Olympics for one hundred years.

Then came the pommel horse event. Nineteen years of hard work and training in the gym had led Louis to this point. He couldn't fail now, could he? As he had done in Beijing, he sat down in a quiet corner with his T-shirt over his head, focusing on the task.

Eventually, he was called. He looked up and saw his name on the screen. The big red dot beside it turned to green, meaning it was time for him to jump onto the pommel horse.

He felt from the start that it was going well. As he turned on the pommel horse he knew that he was in the middle of his best routine ever.

When the scores flashed up Louis' matched that of Krisztián Berki: 16.066! The judges looked at the different parts of the scores. Louis had

scored higher marks for his brilliant routine, but Krisztián Berki had scored better marks for execution. Under the rules of gymnastics, marks for execution outweigh marks for routine. Krisztián Berki got gold. Louis got silver.

Louis was thrilled to get his second medal of the 2012 Olympics, but he had been so close to getting gold. Deep down, though, he felt proud.

Louis had dared to dream to win. He had achieved his dream, becoming the first British male gymnast for one hundred years to win an Olympic medal. Not only that, he had also created a legacy. His historic achievements on the pommel horse would inspire a generation of younger British gymnasts to dream to win.

Fact file
Louis Smith

Full name: Louis Antoine Smith

Born: 22 April 1989, Peterborough, England

Height: 1.79 metres

Major Medals

2006 Commonwealth Games (Melbourne)

Gold — Pommel Horse

Bronze — Team

2007 World Championships (Stuttgart)

Bronze — Pommel Horse

2008 Olympic Games (Beijing)

Bronze — Pommel Horse — the first British man to win a medal in the individual gymnastics for 100 years

2009 European Championships (Milan)

Silver — Pommel Horse

2010 World Championships (Rotterdam)

Silver — Pommel Horse

2010 European Championships (Birmingham)

Silver — Pommel Horse

Silver — Team

2011 World Championships (Tokyo)

Bronze — Pommel Horse

2012 European Championships (Montpellier)

Gold — Team

Silver — Pommel Horse

2012 Olympic Games (London)

Silver — Pommel Horse

Bronze — Team

2014 Commonwealth Games (Glasgow)

Gold — Team

Bronze — Pommel Horse

Other Honours

2013 Appointed Member of the Order of the British Empire (MBE)

Catch up with all the latest news about Louis at:
www.louissmith.com

NICOLA
ADAMS

Roy Apps

DREAM
TO
WIN

EDGE

Nicola Adams

At the Sports Centre, Nicola's mum went off to her aerobics class while her brother Kurtis quickly found his way to football training. A sports coach came over to Nicola.

"What about you, young lady?" he asked. "What would you like to have a go at? Dance, perhaps?"

Nicola frowned and shook her head. "I want to do boxing," she said.

"Boxing?" the coach repeated with a snort. "You're a girl! Girls don't box..." Then he saw the determined look on Nicola's face. He knew straight away it would be no good arguing with her.

Continue reading this story in:
DREAM TO WIN:
Nicola Adams

Tom Daley

Tom stood there, amazed, watching the divers jumping into the water. His mum came up to him.

"Aren't you going on the inflatables, Tom?" she asked.

Tom shook his head.

"What about the water slide, then?"

Tom shook his head again.

"So what do you want to do?"

"That," declared Tom, pointing to the next diver preparing to jump off the 10-metre platform, the highest of them all.

Continue reading this story in:
DREAM TO WIN:
Tom Daley